Veterans Memorial Park
WALL SOUTH

Art Giberson

ISBN-10: 1505823927
ISBN-13: 978-1505823929

Front cover design: Bethany Murray
Back cover: Art Giberson

DEDICATION

Dedicated to the memory of all veterans and their families, but particularly to the 58,272 men and women listed on the black granite panels of Wall South as KIA or MIA from the Vietnam War

CONTENTS

ACKNOWLEDGMENTS

A special thanks to Allen Jones
for the use of his magnificent photos used for the front cover
www.photographybyallenjones.com;
and Bethany Murray for her awe-inspiring skill in designing the cover
and a special thanks to Lieutenant Colonel David Glassman, USMC, Ret. for his faith and
encouragement and Tony Giberson for his assistance
and guidance in producing this second pictorial history of
Wall South/Veterans Memorial Park.

THE MOVING WALL

The creation of WALL SOUTH developed over a period of five years, beginning with a suggestion by Vietnam veterans Lenny Collins and Nelson Wellborn, that a permanent Vietnam Veterans Memorial be constructed in Pensacola Florida after the MOVING WALL, a half-size replica of the Washington, DC Vietnam Veterans Memorial, made a five-day visit to Pensacola in December 1987. From that suggestion the Wall South Foundation was created to pursue funding and selection of a suitable site.

The MOVING WALL came about after Vietnam veteran, John Devitt, attended the 1982 dedication of the Vietnam Veterans Memorial in Washington. The positive power of "The Wall," according to the Moving Wall website, was so strong that Devitt felt the experience should be shared with fellow Vietnam veterans all across the country that may never have the opportunity to visit the national memorial in Washington. With the assistance of fellow Vietnam veteran volunteers, a half-size replica of the memorial they called, The MOVING WALL was built. It was viewed for the first time in Tyler, Texas, in October 1984 and has been touring the country ever since. Unbeknownst to anyone at the time, that portable memorial would be the catalyst for WALL SOUTH and the eventual creation of Pensacola, Florida's Veterans Memorial Park.

In the winter of 1987, a small veterans origination known as, Vietnam Veterans of Northwest Florida, arranged for the portable half-scale replica of the Vietnam Veterans Memorial, to make a stop in Pensacola

Day and night for five days, Vietnam veterans, many of whom were survivors of some of the bloodiest battles of the Vietnam War—Con Thien, Khe Sanh, Cua Viet, Hue, Ky Phu, Monkey Mountain, Hamburger Hill, Chu Lai and Ia Drang— former POWs, family members and friends of those listed on the Wall, stood and stared in awe at the row upon row of white names engraved on the reflective black surface of the Moving Wall.

Others gently touched the name of a loved one and traced the letters with a finger tip. Emotions flowed freely that night, as Pensacola area Vietnam veterans responded to a silent challenge issued by their brothers on the Wall.

On that cold December night, the challenge was accepted and just as they had done nearly two decades before; in the jungles and rice paddies, in the air and on the waters of Southeast Asia, these warriors came together for a final mission—the building of WALL SOUTH.

The Moving Wall brought many Northwest Florida Vietnam veterans together for the first time. Until this half-scale replica of the National Vietnam Veterans Memorial came to the Gulf Coast, most Pensacola and Northwest Florida Vietnam veterans had kept their emotions locked away, hidden from themselves and their families. The Moving Wall changed all that and allowed the veterans, for the first time, to get in touch with their emotions... each in their own way.

By the hundreds, Vietnam veterans, families of deceased veterans, and curious spectators crowed into Seville Square in downtown Pensacola. They touched the names on the portable memorial and vowed to build a memorial in Pensacola...The Gateway to the Sunshine State.

On the Moving Wall's final night in Pensacola, a candle light vigil was held in honor of the more than 58,000 Americans who never returned from Southeast Asia. Veterans and their families gathered to pay their respects one last time before the "Wall" moved on. For one tearful

Vietnam veteran, former Marine Corps Lance Corporal Lenny Collins, saying good-bye to his fellow warriors whose names were inscribed on the black plexiglas panels was especially painful.

"There's something magic here," he proclaimed. "What else could create this kind of emotion?"

Collins, who had served with the 3rd Marine Division, 5th Com., returned home to his native Pittsburgh from Vietnam in 1971. He was anxious to get on with his life and settle down with his wife, Gloria. Unfortunately, Lenny, like many returning Vietnam vets quickly discovered that life would never again be the same.

Unsure of how he would react to society after the horror and brutality of Vietnam, and feeling guilty because he had survived while many of his high school classmates were killed in Vietnam, the former Marine Corps lance corporal retreated into a shell of depression, refusing to leave the house for more than year.

The strain was beginning to take its toll on both Lenny and Gloria, when Lenny received a phone call from a fellow Marine he had become close friends with in Vietnam. That friend, Rusty Davis, asked the Collins' to visit him and his wife in Florida. They accepted the invitation and six days later bought the house next door to Davis.

Surrounded by new friends, in a new location, Collins started to emerge from his shell. On the surface, all appeared perfectly normal. Lenny had completely erased Vietnam from his memory. When filling out job applications or other official forms he routinely wrote "None" in the block that asked about military service. For Lenny Collins, now the father of two daughters and a successful businessman, life was about as good as it could get.

Other than a few close friends, such as Davis and a Navy buddy from his hometown, George Drobnack, he had made no contact with other Vietnam veterans since returning home more than a decade before.

When the Moving Wall was set up in Seville Square on December 7, 1987, Drobnack talked Collins into going with him to see the memorial. "We owe it to our friends and classmates that didn't come back," Drobnack insisted.

As the two friends approached Seville Square that evening, a slight drizzle was falling and the sorrowful sound of Taps, played by a bugler from the Pensacola Naval Air Station, filled the cool evening air. The park, decorated with red ribbons for the holidays and a light mist in the air, created an eerie hypnotic glow over the park and the black V-shaped object that had been placed there. For the first time in years, Lenny Collins thought about the friends he had left in Vietnam.

Reluctant to venture into the park, Collins sat down on the steps of a small restaurant across the street, totally oblivious to the tears flowing freely down his cheeks. A restaurant patron observed him for a few moments and then set down beside him, she too was crying.

"I lost a brother in Vietnam," she told the tearful Marine veteran, "but I can't bear to go over there and look for his name. I'm afraid the emotional strain would just be too much," she told Collins.

The two talked for about an hour and finally decided that no matter how painful it might be, they had to visit the memorial. That short walk across the street changed Lance Corporal Lenny Collins' life. For the first time he realized that he wasn't the only Vietnam veteran who had gone through a period of denial. Every veteran he talked with that night said pretty much the same thing... they had all been riding an emotional roller coaster since returning to "The World." The Moving Wall showed them that while memories of Vietnam and the friends they had lost there were painful; it was something they would have to deal with if they expected to resume any resemblance of a normal life.

The night before the Wall was scheduled to leave Pensacola, Vietnam Veterans of Northwest Florida staged a candlelight vigil. As Collins later describe it, the emotion was overwhelming. People from throughout the area, veterans and non-veterans, stand around openly weeping. Turning to his wife, Gloria, Collins said "We need something like this in Pensacola, there's something magic here. What else could create this kind of raw emotion?"

"You're right," a gentleman standing next to them said, and handed Lenny his card. "Call me after the holidays and we'll talk about it." Collins thanked the stranger and put the card in his pocket without bothering to look at the name.

With the Wall gone and the holidays descending upon him, Collins felt himself slipping back into a state of depression. Then, sometime in January 1988, he remembered the card he had been given. He dug it out and read the name. "Mayor Vince Whibbs." He called the mayor and set up an appointment to talk with him about the possibility of creating a Vietnam Veterans Memorial in Pensacola. Mayor Whibbs, a World War II veteran, was supportive, but concerned about gaining public support for a memorial dedicated to only one group of veterans. The City Council, he suggested, might be more receptive to donating land for an "All Veterans Park."

Pensacola area Vietnam veterans were quick to lend a hand in erecting panels of the Moving Wall in Pensacola's Seville Square when it arrived in Pensacola on December 7, 1987.

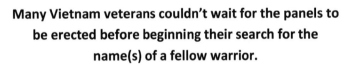

Many Vietnam veterans couldn't wait for the panels to be erected before beginning their search for the name(s) of a fellow warrior.

Helpful volunteers with the Moving Wall project were on hand with a roster showing the location of names on the Moving Wall.

Finding the name of a friend was often painful and required a few moments for saying goodbye and regaining one's composure

For Five days in December 1987, thousands of visitors from throughout Northwest Florida, Southern Alabama and Mississippi converged on Seville Square in downtown Pensacola to pay their respects and leave artifacts at the Moving Wall.

POLITICS VS REALITY

Once the Moving Wall had departed the City of Five Flags, Collins, the gung-ho Marine that he was, suddenly found himself confronted with the first of many major obstacles he and his fellow Vietnam Veterans would have to overcome before their dream of a Pensacola Vietnam Veterans Memorial could become reality. It was obvious that a delicate balance between emotion and political reality would have to be maintained.

A couple of weeks after the Moving Wall departed, Collins attended his first Vietnam Veterans of Northwest Florida (VVNF) meeting and proposed building a replica of the Vietnam Veterans Memorial in Pensacola.

After listening to his proposal, VVNF initiated a committee, co-chaired by Collins and another Vietnam veteran, Nelson Wellborn—who had also proposed building a memorial in honor of Vietnam veterans in Pensacola—to do a study and recommend a possible location for a memorial.

The committee (Lenny & Gloria Collins, Nelson Wellborn, Frank & Marilyn Smith, Richard Hood, William Davis, Bob & Liz Meadows, Al Meadows, Bill & Roseanne Taylor, Micky Reade, Dan Verones, John & Connie Rahn, Leonard Collins, Sr., William Corbin, Butch & Mary Bowling, Kathy Davis, George Drobnack, John Panyko, James Flowers, Mike Thorton, William Polakawicz, , Butch Cook, Anne Hart and Art Giberson) unanimously adopted the idea for a replica of the national Vietnam Veterans Memorial which they would call..."WALL SOUTH."

Collins and Wellborn, who had lost a leg in Vietnam, next approached the city and requested permission to build the memorial in a popular city park. Although the proposed site was very scenic and close to where the Moving Wall had been, it was too small for the proposed memorial.

After some debate, the city council recommended a former minor league baseball park less than a mile away, as an alternative site. In the meantime the veterans commenced holding a series of fund raising events. Because of the illegalities involved in fund raising and acquiring tax exempt status, the VVNF Wall South Committee, soon evolved into the Wall South Foundation and fund-raising was set in motion. Ironically, at the time, no one had a clue as to how much money would eventually be needed or what the memorial would be constructed of.

Although their plans were far from perfect, some would even say haphazard or non-existent, Vietnam Veterans of Northwest Florida stubbornly refused to lose sight of their objective to build a memorial to honor the sacrifices made by their fellow warriors in Vietnam and Southeast Asia.

As the weeks turned into months, goals and fundraising expectations became more realistic and detailed plans began to emerge. Now the vets realized that it was going to be a continuing uphill struggle but they never lost faith that the dream of WALL SOUTH would eventually become reality.

To assist with fund raising and spreading the word about WALL SOUTH a float, designed and built by Vietnam Veterans of Northwest Florida, became a popular attraction in area parades and benefits all along the Gulf Coast. The float, generally manned by one or more combat veterans, was decorated with a mockup of the Vietnam Veterans Memorial, an M-16 topped with a helmet, an American flag and white crosses— one for each year of American involvement in Southeast Asia.

Vietnam veterans would stand at attention and salute when the float passed, civilians and veterans of other wars would bow their heads or place their hands over their heart.

Decorated with a mockup of the Vietnam Veterans Memorial, an M-16 topped with a helmet, an American flag and white crosses, the Vietnam Veterans of Northwest Florida float was a huge attraction in area parades. Vietnam veterans would stand at attention and salute when the float passed; veterans of other wars bowed their heads or placed their hands over their heart.

With fund-raising activities in full swing, two Pensacola area night clubs, Trader Jon's and Terry's Carousel, agreed to host special benefits with live entertainment and donate a percentage of the proceeds to the WALL SOUTH project. With funds slowly coming in and armed with an agreement from the City of Pensacola to donate a five and one-half acre parcel of land (Admiral Mason Park) formerly used as a minor league baseball park for the construction of a veterans park, members of Vietnam Veterans of Northwest Florida gathered at the site on Pensacola's Bayfront Parkway on a blistery cold January day in 1991 and quickly erected a sign proclaiming the site as the future home of WALL SOUTH.

On a blustery January day in 1991 VVNF members and volunteers gathered at the site of a former minor league baseball park to erect a sign proclaiming the location as the future home of WALL SOUTH .

Over the course of the next year, VVNF members washed cars, held road blocks, sold T-shirts, put on concerts and sponsored a variety of other activities to try and raise the estimated one million dollars it would take to build WALL SOUTH

Collins and Wellborn held numerous meetings with local and state elected officials to outline their proposal and solicit their support. A few government officials, including a retired naval officer, were opposed to the idea, but most, like Mayor Whibbs and Florida State Senator W.C. Childers, were very supportive.

"Vietnam veterans," Senator Childers, reportedly told his fellow legislators, "have made a great sacrifice for Florida and the nation. They shouldn't have to stand on street corners, hold car washes and pass the hat to raise money for a memorial."

The Senator then asked the Florida Legislature to appropriate $1.1 million for the construction of a Veterans Memorial Park, featuring WALL SOUTH and later be expanded to include memorials honoring veterans from past and future conflicts. Once approval had been given by the city for Vietnam Veterans of Northwest Florida to build Veterans Memorial Park, high school students and artists, using the National Vietnam Veterans Memorial as an example, produced models and paintings of their vision of what WALL SOUTH would eventually look like.

The paintings and models proved to be a tremendous help in fund raising. While Pensacola area Vietnam veterans could easily envision what the memorial would look like, this marked the first time that visual images were placed before the public. And, while there were several attractive designs available, one produced by four Escambia High School students (Rich Beecher, Eric Bailey, Rusty Westhoff and Randall Smith) came the closest to what the park would eventually look like.

Near the end of the school year in 1990, the four young designers presented their 30-inch by 36-inch model— which took more than 50 hours to build—to the Wall South Foundation for public display at benefits and other fund raising functions.

"It's part of our duty to recognize our veterans," said Rusty Westhoff one of the young designers, and the son of a Vietnam veteran.

Escambia High School students, Rich Beecher, Eric Bailey, Rusty Westhoff and Randall Smith present their WALL SOUTH Model to memorial founders Nelson Wellborn and Lenny Collins.

A painting, completed a couple years earlier by Pensacola artist Pearl Peterson, roughly showing what the park might look like when finished, also provided a big boost in the fund raising project.

On Veterans Day 1991, Vietnam Veterans of Northwest Florida, government officials and numerous community leaders interested in memorializing the memories of the men and women who served in Southeast Asia, gathered at the one-time baseball park for a formal ground-breaking ceremony. Vietnam Veterans of Northwest Florida were finally on the threshold of realizing their dream —building a permanent Vietnam Veterans Memorial in the Western Gateway to the Sunshine State.

On Veterans Day 1991, Vietnam Veterans of Northwest Florida, local and state government officials gathered at the one-time baseball park for a formal ground-breaking

CONSTRUCTION

Actual construction on Veterans Memorial Park/WALL SOUTH began during the first week of June 1992. While Vietnam veterans had always been optimistic about the eventual reality of their memorial, funding continued to be a major stumbling block. That final obstacle was lifted when the Wall South Foundation was notified that the State of Florida, thanks to Senator Childers, would provide $1.4 million to help build the park.

The Vietnam Veterans of Northwest Florida, through T-shirt sales, car washes, concerts and benefits, had already raised $200,000. At a June 4, press conference, called to announce the start of construction, members of the Wall South Foundation and architects from Baskerville-Donovan Engineers, project managers, optimistically proclaimed that WALL SOUTH would be ready for unveiling on October 24, despite the fact, that other than the ground breaking, not a single shovel of dirt had been turned.

WALL SOUTH officials also used the press conference to announce that a World War I Monument located on Garden Street in the heart of Pensacola would be relocated to Veterans Park, and eventually, monuments from other wars could be added. The only thing that could possibly stop the construction of WALL SOUTH now was the weather. Meteorology was suddenly a major topic of discussion for Pensacola area Vietnam veterans.

Once construction got started workmen were under constant pressure to complete the job as soon as possible. Dozens of construction workers, many of whom had either personally served in Vietnam or had family members who did, labored tirelessly to complete work on what they considered a memorial to themselves.

Marine Corps combat veterans Frank Smith, left, and Bill Davis raise the Stars and Stripes over Veterans Memorial Park for the first time

With the raising of the American flag over the park for the first time by two original WALL SOUTH committee members, Frank Smith and Bill Davis, veterans breathed a sigh of relief. The memorial honoring their fallen fellow warriors was nearing completion.

The arrival of the first few WALL SOUTH panels drew a small number of spectators, mostly Vietnam veterans, who gathered at the former baseball park to "supervise" the off-loading of the shiny black panels from trucks. Over the next few days, as new panels were added to the V-shaped structure, more and more people visited the construction site to watch a wood and concrete frame be transformed into a memorial.

Workmen use great care in unloading the panels for WALL SOUTH

As the black granite panels were hung into place, area veterans and other citizens scanned the row upon row of names, hoping to find the name of a fellow warrior or loved one. Although there were obviously much to be done and precious little time before the planned dedication ceremony, spirits soared to ever higher heights with the hanging of each panel.

With only slightly more than a week to spare, the first ten panels of WALL SOUTH arrived at the construction site and were quickly off loaded and prepared for placement on the wall's foundation.

Despite a steady stream of spectators searching for names, the pace of construction never wavered. Ingram employees, like Vietnam Veterans of Northwest Florida had accepted a challenge and they too, were determined to see it completed on time.

Workmen, particularly those from Ingram Memorial Company, the firm responsible for the panels, were under intense pressure to finish the memorial in the few days remaining before the scheduled October 24 dedication.

Ingram employees seemed to excel under the increased pressure of an impending deadline and worked late into the night to have everything ready. Despite their skills and dedication, several of the 32 panels which would make up WALL SOUTH didn't arrive until after the formal dedication.

Although each panel was hung with great care, the first received extra special attention. This panel, much like the first troops to land in Vietnam in March 1965, set the stage for the ones to follow. Exact measurements were required to ensure that each succeeding panel would line up correctly.

While each of Ingram's workers, some of whom were Vietnam veterans, had a keen interest in ensuring each panel was exact, one in particular, James D. Mosley, had a very special interest. For Mosley the opportunity to help erect WALL SOUTH provided a strange and unique opportunity to be reunited with fallen warriors he had known only through death.

Mosley had been responsible for sending the remains of many of those listed on the black granite panels of WALL SOUTH home. For most of his tour in Vietnam in 1969 the former Army specialist was assigned to the mortuary at Da Nang.

When Mosley found out that his company had been contracted to install the panels he asked to be assigned to the job. "This is a special honor for me," Mosley said. "If the body of an American trooper came through the Da Nang mortuary I probably had something to do with sending the remains home. I've never seen the Wall in Washington so this job gave me the opportunity to pay my respects."

Although Mosley didn't remember the names of most of those he sent home, there was, nevertheless, a special bond between him and those listed on WALL SOUTH. His strongest emotions flooded to the surface when he erected panel Number One, with the phrase...

"Dear Lord and Father of the universe, help us to never forget the sacrifices these brothers and sisters, whose names are upon this wall gave for us all"... inscribed in the upper left corner.

With the installation of each new panel more and more visitors flocked to the park site to search for names. At times construction workers were forced to work around spectators. Although they could have easily put the construction site off limits, they never did so. Because they too, had friends and family members listed on the wall and they understood the public's anxieties.

As the panels were going up and last minute adjustments were being made to other sections of the park, Vietnam veterans, Boy Scouts, private citizens, and host of other volunteers donated their time to lay sod on the bare sandy ground.

The names on the panels of WALL SOUTH held a very special meaning for James D. Mosley.

With less than 24-hours to go, veterans and local citizens, worked at a feverish pace to get the last square of sod into place. As the volunteers labored in the 85 degree mid-October heat, helicopters from nearby Whiting Field Naval Air Station, practiced the flyover they would perform the next day. The helicopters would approach WALL SOUTH from the southeast—the direction of Vietnam—and fly over the wall, signaling the release of a curtain which had been draped over the wall during the dedication speeches.

Long before the dedication, however, visitors were already leaving flowers and mementos at the base of the panels.

As the clock ticked off the final few hours before Dedication Day, Vietnam Veterans of Northwest Florida gathered at the WALL for the cremation of a copy of the book listing the names of those who failed to return from Southeast Asia. The day after the dedication, several VVNF members boarded a Coast Guard patrol boat with the ashes from that book, along with a wreath, containing notes and photographs, placed at WALL SOUTH during the dedication, and dropped them in the Gulf of Mexico.

It was their belief that the ashes, wreath and notes from loved ones, would spread across the waters and be carried by the winds, to the shores of Vietnam where their fellow warriors, husbands, brothers and sisters, sons and daughters served and died, or remained unaccounted for.

Television Personality Sue Straughn assists VVNF members with the symbolic cremation ceremony of the book listing the names of those who failed to return from Vietnam

Roster book ashes, a wreath containing notes and photographs, are dropped in the Gulf of Mexico for a symbolic voyage back to Vietnam

As Pensacola area veterans fought to beat the clock, VVNF/Wall South Foundation officials interrupted their chores to welcome an unexpected visitor, Vice Presidential Candidate Al Gore to Veterans Memorial Park.

Gore, a former Army journalist who served in Vietnam, was in the Florida Panhandle on a campaign tour and stopped by the park, unannounced, to show his respects to two high school classmates listed on the wall.

Vice Presidential Candidate Al Gore, locates the name of a high school classmate killed in Vietnam. Below: The future Vice President locates the name of another classmate.

A rose colored sky proclaims a new day
The Florida sun burns the mist off the bay

Memorial Park's lawn is still wet with dew, the WALL SOUTH takes on a pinkish hue.

A lone figure kneels at the base of the Wall, the faces are easily recalled. The names are listed in the order they died, So those who died together are listed side by side.

His fingers trace the grooves of each and every name of the buddies he saw the night Charlie came to call.

One by one his pals went down, as Charlie walked in the mortar rounds.

The mortars were followed by ground attack

Finally, at dawn, Charlie pulled back.

By then no souls were left, save one to feel the warmth of the Asian sun.

A generation later, our hero feels shame, for surviving the night Charlie came

But the Ghosts of his buddies blame him not

They swelled with pride when he fired the last shot

Pensacola wakens to another day But one man's mind is far away, Saturday shoppers head for the mall while a lonely figure kneels at the base of the Wall.

Sgt. R.N. Alden 11th Pathfinders, 1st Air Cavalry Division,

DEDICATION DAY
OCTOBER 24, 1992

The dream of a memorial in honor of Vietnam veterans in Pensacola became reality at 11a.m, October 24, 1992, as thousands of people from around the nation gathered for the dedication of WALL SOUTH and the transformation of a former baseball park into hallowed ground.

As each significant event detailing the long road to this day was revealed, and names read, the mellow tones of a bell drafted out across Pensacola Bay as though calling the warriors listed on the wall home for this special occasion. Many of the Vietnam veterans gathered for the dedication stood and stared in awe at what had been accomplished.

"It's like I went to sleep and woke up living in a real live dream. Today, WALL SOUTH is real," proclaimed a weeping vet.

As each of the more than 58,000 names was called, a bell was rung in their honor.

October 1992, even by Florida standards, was unusually warm, but hot or cold; rain or shine, spirits were high—it was WALL SOUTH dedication day.

Hours before the official dedication ceremony was scheduled to begin, the crowd, which would eventually grow to more than 50,000, started pouring onto the five and one half acre site overlooking Pensacola Bay. They came by car, on motorcycles, on foot and as members of various bands and marching groups.

It was time to renew old acquaintances. To reunite with buddies last seen in the rice paddies and jungles, or on the waters in and around Vietnam. These men and women, veterans of an unpopular war, stood transfixed in the blazing sun waiting for the unveiling of their memorial. A memorial they had built unto themselves and their comrades in arms whose names were engraved on the black granite panels.

Vietnam POW and former U.S. Senator Rear Admiral Jeremiah Denton; U.S. Congressman Earl Hutto; Florida State Senator W.D. Childers; Vietnam veteran and (then) Pensacola Mayor Jerry Maygarden; spoke in turn as the ever growing crowd waited inpatiently.

The moment they had come for was at hand. As each speaker ended his speech thousands of eyes turned toward "The Wall."

Thousands of people from throughout the Florida Panhandle, neighboring states and across the nation, mustered in Pensacola on October 24, 1992 to witness history being made with the unveiling of WALL SOUTH

The long, five year battle was over. Vietnam Veterans of Northwest Florida had completed the challenge issued by their colleagues on the silk-screened panels of the Moving Wall that cold December night in 1987.

Vietnam veterans from across the Southeast stood transfixed awaiting the unveiling of their memorial—WALL SOUTH

Although conceived and built to honor those who made the ultimate sacrifice in Southeast Asia, WALL SOUTH is also a memorial to the handful of dedicated veterans, notably: *Lenny & Gloria Collins, Nelson Wellborn, Frank & Marilyn Smith, Richard Hood William Davis, Bob & Liz Meadows, Al Meadows, Roseanne & Bill Taylor, Micky Reade, Dan Verones, John &Connie Rahn, Leonard Collins, Sr, William Corbin, Butch & Mary Bowling, Kathy Davis, George Drobnack, John Panyko, James Flowers, William Polakawicz, Mike Thorton, Butch Cook and Anne Hart* who refused to give up on a pledge to keep the memories of their buddies and family members alive.

The grounds of the former minor league baseball park literally shook from the applause of more than 50,000 people when VNNF President Lenny Collins announced;
"Unveil WALL SOUTH!"

Even though they had been asked to wait until the drape covering the memorial was fully raised, thousands of people instantly began edging closer to the black V-shaped object as Navy helicopters flew overhead.

A helicopters flyover and release of white doves signified that WALL SOUTH was at last a reality

The first dedication guest to officially locate a name on WALL SOUTH

was Mrs. Alice White Ferrell.

Mrs. Ferrell's 19-year-old son, Chris Roger Behm, was killed in Vietnam on September 30, 1971. Mrs. Ferrell WALL SOUTH's Gold Star Mother, was escorted to the wall by one of the founding fathers of the Vietnam Veterans of Northwest Florida, Mickey Reade, who assisted her in locating Chris' name on panel N1, line 17.

After helping the Gold Star Mother locate her son's name Vietnam veteran and one of the founders of WALL SOUTH, Micky Reade, (above) gave Mrs. Ferrell a red rose which she gently placed on her son's name (below right) and she quietly whispered,

"Welcome Home, Chris."

When the Gold Star Mother was finished, Lenny Collins made the announcement that everyone was waiting to hear.

"The Memorial is now open to the public"

Instantly a near stampede nearly took place as thousands of people rushed toward the shiny black panels, which from that moment on would forever be known by one and all as: WALL SOUTH.

With veterans, many disabled with wounds from the war, leading the way a mass of humanity rushed to find the name of a loved one on WALL SOUTH

The search for a name on WALL SOUTH began with standing in long lines and scanning thousands of names on a computer printout. Though the war had been over for nearly 20 years, the families of those still listed as missing had never given up hope. For them, many of whom had only a vague, or no memory at all, of a father, brother or sister, WALL SOUTH brought the spirit of their loved ones home. Once a name was located in the book, visitors had to scan the rows of names on the specified panel and line.

But on this late fall day in 1992, no one seemed to mind the wait or the pain-staking search for a name. The book listing the names was eventually keyed into a computer data base, courtesy of Navy Vietnam veteran Gerald Foote.

Former Navy Corpsman Tom Fournier was among the first wheelchair veterans to reunite with his buddies listed on the WALL

**A former Army nurse helps a blind veteran locate the name
of a fallen friend**

**The WALL SOUTH dedication was a time for old friends, colleagues and
combat veterans to meet again and pay their respects to fallen warriors.**

Searching for a name on WALL SOUTH was hard for veterans and family members alike, actually finding the name, served only to verify the sad fact that a fellow warrior, friend or loved one would never return from Vietnam.

Although it had been rumored for several days that Vice President Dan Quayle would be attending the dedication of WALL SOUTH, he didn't actually arrive until an hour or so after the park had officially opened to the public. In explaining his tardiness to the thousands of veterans and guests gathered for the dedication, the vice president said he had purposely delayed his arrival because this day was reserved for those who had served in Southeast Asia, and politicians had no right to intrude on their special day.

The Vice President thanked Lenny Collins and other VVNF members for their service to the country and unrelenting determination in bringing WALL SOUTH into existence.

After greeting local and state dignitaries, including former POW and U.S. Senator retired Rear Admiral Jeremiah Denton; the Vice President was escorted by Collins and Retired Army Master Sergeant Bill Corbin, to the Wall so he could pay his respects to the more than 58,000 of his fellow Americans listed on the black reflective panels of the memorial.

WALL SOUTH founder Lenny Collins is congratulated by Vice President Dan Quayle for his efforts in the creation of WALL SOUTH.

Vice President Dan Quayle is greeted by WALL SOUTH Master of Ceremonies Master Sgt. Bill Corbin, U.S. Army (Ret.) and Rear Adm. Jeremiah Denton, U.S. Navy (Ret)

Lenny Collins escorts Vice President Dan Quayle during Quayle's visit to WALL SOUTH

WALL SOUTH founder Lenny Collins points out the name of friend killed in Vietnam

FOREVER IN STONE
Loving fingers tenderly trace chiseled names in the granite face

Family and Friends, heartfelt moments alone

Shared memories of those forever in stone

To heal the Wound

To say Goodbye

To touch reality, then to cry.

All this is an answer to those who ask

Why?

Kathleen Collins June 1992

WHY DO I FEAR THE WALL?

To face the Wall, this I fear most of all. A part of me is in the Wall. The Wall lives for all of them, through us.
In our hearts, they'll never die. From the Wall they reach, as if to say, In your hearts, we'll always stay.
Through your love we live today. Through pain and joy, memories and tears. We'll always be there.
Your pain of losing one so dear. The joy we shared, when they were near. The memories are cloudy, sometimes so clear, Even the bad ones, are cherished and dear.
For they are all that I am, and all that you are.
No matter how far or near, always the tears. The betrayal of feelings, we guard so dear. A tear is but a tiny window, to a broken heart and shattered memories.
No, the pain and fear won't go away.
I must face the Wall someday.

John Wayne Harrell

They come from across America.
A pilgrimage to a Wall, a tribute to themselves they made.
Inscribed with names of comrades in battle fell
To black granite and concrete,
are drawn.
With tears in the eyes the past they must face, before a
future to began.
Dressed in worn battle dress fatigues:
Olive drab, jungle garb, adorned with campaign ribbons,
medals, patches of long gone units they come,
to reconcile what they had done.
Professionals and non, fathers, sons and brothers.
They come to find, shipmates soul mates, comrades in
arms,
Acquaintances and strangers, friends they became, a war
fought still unwon

With empty stares they gaze into dark panels reflections.
Younger faces stare back, young men they once were.
For hours it seems, they stand expressionless, as tears well
up on their eyes.

As time goes by, they all reach out,

To touch. Hands to the wall like a magnet to steel.
All feel compelled to touch the names of young men, lost
on foreign shores

Only old warriors remain to carry the pain.

Tony Giberson
Son of a Vietnam Veteran

A VICTORY WON

With the dedication of WALL SOUTH, their mission was complete. For Northwest Florida Vietnam veterans it was time to celebrate their accomplishments. The bands: Britt Small and Festival; Rare Earth; the Bridge Builders Quartet; Terry Thomas and the Carousels; and McGuire's Pipe Band, entertained the veterans and their guests from early afternoon until late into the night.

The night, October 24, 1992, belonged to Pensacola area Vietnam Veterans. They had emerged victoriously from a five year struggle to build a memorial to their fellow warriors. It was now time for rejoicing and dancing in the streets. After five years of heartbreak, sweat and tears, they had earned the right to celebrate.

Their friends on the Wall would have no doubt, nodded their approval. Indeed the presence of those 58,000 plus warriors could be felt throughout the evening. You could almost hear them say, "Drink one for me bro!"

When Britt Small, a Vietnam veteran and band leader who had performed at the dedication of the National Vietnam Veterans Memorial in Washington, DC took the stage, more than 70,000 people rocked the streets of downtown Pensacola. It was a night for celebration. For Northwest Florida area Vietnam veterans, the pledge they had made five years earlier to their brothers and sisters listed on the black shiny panels of the Moving Wall had been successfully carried out.

They had every right to celebrate. They had achieved what few thought was possible. As Lenny Collins so eloquently stated during his dedication speech, "We began this journey, this endeavor, knowing that we alone shared the dream. The dream of a Vietnam Veterans Memorial in Pensacola. First there were seven of us. Then twelve. A ten dollar bill was donated by an Air Force veteran. Then there were fifteen believers and the Wall South Committee was formed. Then we were twenty and we had raised $1,000. Then $2,000 and then $3,000. As the dream grew so did the challenges and the number of obstacles we had to overcome. But in the end we prevailed."

When Britt Small, a Vietnam veteran who had performed at the dedication of the National Vietnam Veterans Memorial dedication in Washington, DC took the stage more than 70,000 people rocked the streets of downtown Pensacola.

On this night, despite the fact, that they had to provide it themselves, Vietnam veterans finally received the long overdue, welcome home, they deserved.

It had indeed been a long, obstacle-laden path; Vietnam Veterans of Northwest Florida had travelled to reach the electrifying mood of sheer enchantment they felt as they celebrated late into the night of October 24, 1992.

But with the coming of the dawn, reality once again surfaced. The objective... building WALL SOUTH had been accomplished, but the mission was far from over. Veterans Day was only eighteen days away and arrangements had to be made for a Veterans Day service to be held at the newly dedicated Veterans Park.

Despite the fact that this was the home of WALL SOUTH it was designed, after all, to be an "all veterans park." While there was no defying the powerful pull of those black granite panels, there had been some opposition to building the wall because many felt it would be unfair to veterans of other wars. VVNF's next objective therefore was to convince their fellow warriors and the citizenry, that while WALL SOUTH was the center piece of what would eventually become known as Veterans Memorial Park, it was a memorial to veterans of all wars. This first ever Veterans Day service at the park was a key feature in showing that this was a memorial for veterans of all American conflicts—past and future.

SPECIAL OCCASIONS

The weather in Northwest Florida can undergo many changes in a period of eighteen days. While dedication day had been sunny and unseasonably warm, November 11, 1992, Veterans Day, was cold with a day-long torrential downpour. Many Veterans Day parades and ceremonies throughout the region were cancelled. WALL SOUTH Veterans Day ceremonies, however, continued as planned.

It would have taken a great deal more than a little rain to keep people from observing Veterans Day 1992 at WALL SOUTH

An overhead statement by a Vietnam veteran, who had been instrumental in the development of WALL SOUTH, put everything in prospective, "The heavens are weeping for our brothers on the WALL."

For those gathered for Veterans Day ceremonies at the newly opened Veterans Park, tears were flowing as freely as the deluge from the heavens. But despite the cold and rain, or perhaps because of it, area veterans and their families seemed to be closer, emotionally, than ever before.

There was no longer any doubt that WALL SOUTH, in only eighteen short days, had been accepted by all as a hallowed and sacred place.

"Standing in the rain is the least we can do for our brothers" said a veteran. "A little rain never stopped us in Nam"

No amount of rain was going to prevent Vietnam vets from paying their respects to those listed on the WALL on the first Veterans Day at WALL SOUTH

The 1992 Christmas holidays would be remembered for a long, long time. It was, after all, Christmas of 1987, when the idea of a Vietnam Veterans Memorial in Pensacola took root. It was an anniversary of sorts, and to celebrate, the builders of WALL SOUTH, in conjunction with Homestead Village, a Pensacola retirement home, set up a Christmas tree and invited the public to decorate it with ornaments bearing the name of one of the more than 58,000 names listed on the Wall. Throughout the holiday period, VVNF members stood a vigil at WALL SOUTH as a way of sharing the Christmas season with those they had served with years before.

On Christmas Day, 1992 more than 1,000 people visited Veterans Memorial Park to spend some time with a loved one, friend, or fellow warrior.

"There are 32 names of men from my old outfit on there," said a retired Army sergeant major, "Christmas just seemed like the appropriate time to visit with them."

Christmas is the perfect time to spend some time with colleagues on the Wall

A PARK FOR ALL OCCASIONS

WALL SOUTH quickly became the preferred setting for military personnel to re-enlist, retire and be awarded medals. In January 1993, Petty Officer First Class Mark C. Lange, a sailor assigned to the Pensacola Naval Air Station, became the first person to re-enlist at WALL SOUTH. Although he was too young to have served in the Vietnam War, Petty Officer Lange chose the memorial for his reenlistment out of respect for those who had went before.

A month later, another first was established at Veterans Park, when Lt. Roger Whetstone, a highly decorated Vietnam veteran requested that his retirement flag be one that had flown over WALL SOUTH.

Petty Officer First Class Mark C. Lange, from the Pensacola Naval Air Station, became the first person to reenlist at WALL SOUTH. His Department Head Lt. Sam Black administered the oath of enlistment

For years retiring military personnel have been presented with a flag flown over the United States Capital and, as much of an honor as that is, Whetstone, who served as a Navy hospital corpsman with the Marines in Vietnam in 1969-1970, felt that a flag flown over WALL SOUTH was an even greater honor.

The ceremonial flag raising and re-enlistment at WALL SOUTH in the first two months of 1993, set the pace for what proved to be an exciting and emotion-filled year for the only permanent Vietnam Veterans Memorial outside the nation's capitol to list the names of all those who never returned from Southeast Asia.

In early March, the remains of Navy Lt. Ralph E. Foulks Jr., an A-4E Skyhawk pilot, shot down on January 5, 1968, were returned to Pensacola for burial at Barrancas National Cemetery.

Vietnam Veterans of Northwest Florida held a 25-hour vigil—one hour for

each year he was missing—at WALL SOUTH in front of Panel 18-S where the lieutenant's name is listed.

Elvah Jones finds the name of her son, Navy Lt. Ralph E. Foulks Jr., on Panel 18-S. Right, a flight helmet and cross bearing the date the lieutenant was shot down was placed in front of the panel where his name is located

This scene was repeated five months later when the remains of Capt. David D. Frederick, a Marine helicopter pilot, were returned to the Cradle of Naval Aviation for burial at Barrancas.

Capt. Frederick and his three crewmen were killed in 1967 when their CH-46 helicopter was downed during a medevac flight. A 26-hour vigil—one hour for each year he was missing—was held at WALL SOUTH.

A midnight change of the vigil guard for Capt. David Frederick at WALL SOUTH

In addition to the thousands of human visitors making an appearance at WALL SOUTH during the first few months of its existence, Mother Nature also decided to visit the park by way of a rare snow storm during the weekend of March 13-14, 1993.

The first measurable snow to fall on Pensacola since January 1977 lightly blanketed the area and provided WALL SOUTH with a surrealistic scene for a short time.

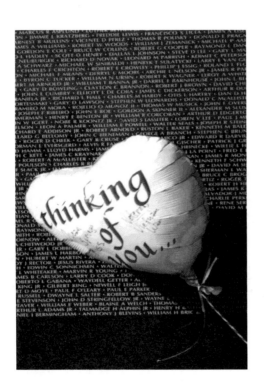

Within a day or so, however, things were back to normal and students from the Naval Technical Training Center at Corry Station—most of whom weren't even born when Lt. Foulks and Capt. Fredericks were killed—

were posing for class pictures at the wall while visitors and veterans continued to visit with friends or search for the name of loved ones listed there.

A graduating class from the Naval Air Technical Training Center choose WALL SOUTH as the backdrop for their class photograph

Even before the memorial was complete, letters, cards and mementos of every description; love letters, birthday cards, sometimes crudely drawn by a small child; birth announcements, photographs and flowers, started showing up at WALL SOUTH.

The mementos included medals, campaign ribbons, military uniform items, such as helmets, flak jackets, boots and full uniforms, POW/MIA bracelets and many personal items: tooth brushes, socks, cigarettes, candy bars and beer—lots of beer.

Each of these items, balloons, notes, letters and cards are special. Exactly why they are left at the WALL is known only to the person who left them. But whatever the reason, it's clear that it's a personal way of communicating with the warriors on the Wall.

WHERE IS MY FATHER?
Cdr. Donald Richard Hubbs
Missing in Vietnam since March 17, 1968

WHAT IS THE UNITED STATES GOVERN
DOING TO LOCATE THIS MAN?

Vietnam veterans believe that the mementos and written messages are merely part of the healing process. Some letters and cards are open, for all to read, others are in sealed envelopes. The sealed envelopes are private conversations and personal thoughts and are never opened by any member of the Vietnam Veterans of Northwest Florida or Wall South Foundation, to open and read these

would be an invasion of privacy. The open letters and cards, on the other hand, are perhaps meant to help people understand the hurt that still lingers these many years after the war in Vietnam ended. A sampling of these open letters runs the gamut from cheerful messages to long pent-up emotions.

"We are always thinking of you, our brother on the Wall. We shared your happiness, your sorrows and many a brew.

Now we share but your memory. That's why we place these wreaths, in your name, at the memorial built to honor you and make rubbings of your name as a keepsake and to share with others."

Although frequently over-shadowed by the black, V shaped Vietnam Veterans Memorial; other memorials also reside in Veterans Memorial Park.

Fittingly, the first addition was the World War I Memorial.

Located on the southwestern end of the park, the white World War I Memorial stands in stark contrast to the black V of the Vietnam Veterans Memorial.

Originally located on Garden Street in the heart of Pensacola, the memorial was relocated with the birth of Veterans Memorial Park. Unfortunately, relocation wasn't as simple as WALL SOUTH founders and their architects had at first believed.

The memorial honoring the veterans of the "War to end all Wars" — World War I —reflected in the panels of WALL SOUTH, serves as reminder that as long as mankind inhabits the earth there will probably always be wars.

Constructed in the early 1920's of sandstone and abused by the elements for nearly three-quarters of a century, the sandstone began to crumble when disturbed. Using the existing memorial as a model, a new World War I Memorial, constructed of white marble, was built at Veterans Memorial Park.

The new memorial, an exact replica of the old, is more visible and visited by more people than ever before.

Like WALL SOUTH, in whose panels the monument's image is reflected, the World War I memorial, stands in silent tribute to those who served when called upon to do so.

From its inception WALL SOUTH has been the site of choice for a variety of events from military reunions to public and military school functions, to weddings.

In May 1993, former Marine Corps Lance Corporal Patrick E.D. McCrary, a Pensacola Postal Service employee, was awarded a Purple Heart at the Wall by Marine Corps Col. Mike J. Cross, for injuries he had received 26 years earlier during a fire fight in the Anhoe Valley area of South Vietnam.

A few days later Pensacola residents Chris and Kimberly Palmsteen said their wedding vows at the Wall. Chris said he and Kimberly chose to be married at the Wall "out of respect for all those who never returned to wed the girl they had left behind."

Former Marine Corps Lance Corporal Patrick E.D. McCrary is awarded the Purple Heart for injuries he had received in 1963.

While formal and informal ceremonies were being conducted at Veterans Memorial Park, visitors, including, the wife of former POW, U.S. Senator John McCain, came from across the nation to stop by the park and spend some time with friends and loved ones, whose spirit resides in the black granite panels of WALL SOUTH.

Pensacola, Florida, with its abundance of naval bases and military support, is known around the world as a prime military reunion site. The construction of WALL SOUTH served to further enhance that reputation, particularly among Vietnam veteran's reunion groups.

The park has also proven to be a popular site for school field trips. "A trip to Veterans Memorial Park provides us an opportunity to show our students the consequence of war," said a middle school teacher.

Students and teachers from Pensacola's Ferry Pass Middle School are given an overview of the Vietnam War and Veterans Park by VVNF volunteers.

Students look for the "Angels on the Wall," nurses killed in Vietnam: Lt. Sharon Lane, USA; Lt. Pamela D. Donovan, USA; Lt. Diane H. Orlowski, USA; Lt. Carol Ann E. Drazba, USA; Lt. Elizabeth Ann Jones, USA; Lt. Col. Annie Ruth Graham, USA; Capt. Eleanor G. Alexander, USA and Capt. Mary K. Klinker, USAF, and make rubbings of their names.

On Veterans Day 1993, a new and practical addition, a UH-1M Huey helicopter, was made to Veterans Memorial Park; courtesy of the U. S. Navy and Helicopter Combat Support Squadron Sixteen (the Bullfrogs) which had been scheduled for decommissioning

The Huey helicopter has been credited with saving thousands of lives in Vietnam and the squadron's commanding officer, a Vietnam veteran who flew in Vietnam, felt it only appropriate that a helicopter synonymous with the war in Southeast Asia be retired at WALL SOUTH.

In keeping with the spirit of naval pride, Seabees from Naval Construction Battalion 402 (CBU-402) based at Pensacola Naval Air Station, transported the helicopter from the Air Station to Veterans Memorial Park and erected it on a pedestal near the north end of WALL SOUTH.

The Huey quickly proved to be a picturesque backdrop for ceremonies and location marker for out of town visitors to the park.

The Huey hovered over WALL SOUTH as a silent sentinel until it was destroyed by Hurricane Ivan in 2004. It was replaced with a Marine Corps

Cobra helicopter in 2007.

Although all veterans' ceremonies at Veterans Memorial Park are conducted out of respect for those who wore the uniform in defense of America, few ceremonies are taken more seriously or more somber than those conducted in observance of POW/MIA Recognition Day.

For 14 years the UH-1M Huey stood as a silent sentinel ready to fly a medevac flight should any of the warriors on the Wall need assistance.

Long before Veterans Memorial Park and WALL SOUTH were completed, veterans, mostly Vietnam veterans, gathered each September to pay tribute not only to their brothers missing in Southeast Asia, but to honor all those who suffered through the ordeal of being a Prisoner of War.

Whenever possible, the featured speaker for these public POW/MIA observances, was one who could speak on the topic with authority—former POWs. Speakers, ranging back to when WALL SOUTH was still but a dream have included former POWs from World War II, Korea, Vietnam, and later, Desert Storm.

But regardless of what conflict they served in, the former POWs have all expressed the same thing, a deep faith in their country and their God. Nearly all have shared stories of unbelievable cruelty and moments of compassion by their captors.

Retired Navy Commander Ralph Gaither, held captive by the North Vietnamese for more than seven years, praised all who those served in Vietnam and the more than 58,000 who are listed on the Wall in particular, during a September 1994 speech at the park.

"They went because they were patriots and felt that it was the right thing to do," he said.

"It seems like only yesterday that I and all us gray-haired guys, and a few ladies, left America for Vietnam. When I learned of Vietnam, I didn't know where it was. I had to look at a map to find out where it was at. I was going through flight training at NAS Pensacola when Lt. (jg) Everett Alvarez, the first naval aviator captured by North Vietnam, was shot down on August 5, 1964 after attacking the naval docks in Hon Gai Harbor.

Twenty-three of my classmates from Miami Edison, Class of 1960, are listed on the Wall.

When we, the Vietnam Veterans of Northwest Florida, decided to hollow this ground, to take the names of all our shipmates who never came home from Southeast Asia, and put them on the wall, as we did in Washington, it was a major step for us. Because we took this ground, which was but a wayside park, where we threw around a few baseballs, and we hallowed it with their blood, their sacrifice, their willingness to go and serve in a country, they probably didn't know where it was either. But they stood up for the values that you and I know that America has to stand for in order to continue to be a great country— the values of right and wrong, of liberty, and the pursuit of happiness.

We went to Vietnam, to give them the same freedoms that we enjoy, that our forefathers gave us. It wasn't ours, to question why, but rather to go and do our job. And we did our job well. We won every battle we fought. But when it was all said and done we were told that we had lost.

We're here tonight, on new ground, and this is new ground in Pensacola, and forever it will be, for as long as you and I and the memories of these people listed on the WALL survive.

I thank all of you, my buddies, who built this park. You worked hard; you held fish fries, runs, sold T-shirts and did hundreds of other things to build this park. Now we have it. It's a tangible symbol of the love we have for those we served with and never returned."

Retired Navy Commander Ralph Gaither, with the Huey Helicopter as a backdrop, addresses the audience at a 1994 POW/MIA ceremony at Veterans Memorial Park.

One of those heroes the commander was speaking of is Medal of Honor recipient retired Army Chief Warrant Officer Mike Novosel.

The Army flyer was awarded the nation's highest medal for rescuing 29 wounded soldiers near the Cambodian border in 1969.

Assigned to the Naval Support Facility, Vung Tau, South Vietnam, CWO-4 Novosel was just completing a seven hour dustoff (medevac) mission on October 2, 1969, when he received an urgent call to evacuate an Army unit pinned down and surrounded by enemy forces near the Cambodian border.

Arriving on scene a few minutes later, Novosel's HU-1 Huey came under intense ground fire as he landed and took the first nine wounded men aboard. After flying them to safety he returned to the area and took out another nine.

On the third and final flight into the hostile zone, Warrant Officer Novosel, his crew, and the last of the men he had come to rescue, narrowly missed becoming names on the Wall.

As the last man was being pulled aboard, a Viet Cong stepped out of the bushes not more than 30 feet in front of the helicopter and commenced

Retired Army Chief Warrant Officer Mike J. Novosel was awarded the nation's highest award for a daring rescue under enemy fire which put him and his crew in grave danger.

spraying AK-47 rounds at the cockpit. Novosel was hit in the hand and foot, but still held his position until the last man was aboard before lifting off.

In recognition of his heroic actions and superior airmanship in rescuing 29 of his fellow warriors, Warrant Officer Novosel was awarded the Medal of Honor.

Small white crosses are sometimes placed in front of the WALL SOUTH during special ceremonies—one cross for each year Americans died in Southeast Asia.

May 29, 1995 marked the third and possibly the most (until that time) significant Memorial Day observance to be held at Veterans Memorial Park. It was the unveiling of 13 new names which had been added to WALL SOUTH a few days earlier.

A small number of Wall South Foundation members gathered at WALL SOUTH in May 1995 to witness the engraving of 13 new names on the wall by workers from Ingram Memorial Company, the same company who installed the panels on WALL SOUTH three years earlier.

The new names: PFC James J. Byszek, USA; Sgt. Charles L. Colleps, USA; Pvt. Robert G. Humphreys, USA; Sgt. Donald E. Kramei; USA; PO3 Donald D. Maki, USN; Spec. Michael J. Rowcroft, USA; Master Sgt. Mateo Sabog, USA; Lt. Frank S. Crismon, USN; SSgt Francis P. Jelinek, USA; SP4 Lee R. Schaaf, USA; PFC Thomas L. Gates, USA; PO2 Robert H. Holloway, USN; SP4 Douglas E. Peterson, USA, were warriors who died of combat related wounds while being treated at hospitals outside of Vietnam.

What started as a gesture of respect to fallen comrades in arms, soon turned into a massive magnet drawing together veterans from all walks of life. Strangers who shared but a single common link—service in the Armed Forces of the United States, during America's most controversial armed conflict.

The building of WALL SOUTH made friends of those strangers, and reunited them with the reflections on the Wall—Reflections of themselves. They were together then. And they are together again.

Sculptor Randy New, shows his daughter Savanna, the final mold for his Children's Homecoming Memorial statue.

From the very beginning, the founders of WALL SOUTH had envisioned a veteran's park with memorials honoring veterans of all wars. Gradually, over the years, new memorials were added to Veterans Memorial Park, the first major addition was a Children's Homecoming Memorial dedicated on Veterans Day 2000.

Randy New a local art teacher and sculptor, the creator of the memorial, was only five-years old when his father was killed in Vietnam. His sculpture, a bronze statue of a little girl, is dedicated to all children who lost their father in Vietnam.

A World War II Memorial designed by retired Navy Captain Robert Rasmussen

followed on Veterans Day 2002.

The Children's Homecoming Memorial features a little girl holding a doll in one hand and an American flag in the other, who appears to be waiting for a grandfather she never knew.

This memorial, also initially met with some skepticism.

Despite the fact that the memorial features five life-size statues representing the men and women from each branch of the armed forces that severed during World War II. In the beginning, some members of the Coast Guard felt that their service wasn't equally represented until it was pointed out that during World War II, the Coast Guard served as part of the U.S. Navy. Thus, the sailor featured on the memorial represented both the Navy and Coast Guard equally. Once this had been pointed out, mostly by World War II era Coast Guardsmen, it was clear sailing and all branches accepted the memorial as their own.

In October 2002, a month before the planned dedication of the World War II memorial, film makers Patrick and Cheryl Fries, producers of a documentary about the HU-2 Huey helicopter and the role it played in Vietnam, titled, *In the Shadow of the Blade,* made a stop at WALL SOUTH as part of an eight state Landing Zones tour.

At each stop interviews were conducted with Vietnam veterans from all branches of the military. Each flight leg carried Vietnam War veterans. The documentary's "mission of healing and reconciliation" lifted off at Fort Rucker, Alabama, where many Vietnam helicopter pilots trained before deployment. Vietnam War journalist Joseph L. Galloway, author of the bestselling book, *We Were Soldiers Once . . . and Young,* spoke at the ceremonial event, after which veteran Huey pilot, Medal of Honor recipient Chief Warrant Officer Michael J. Novosel, with a crew of Vietnam veterans representing the United States Army, Marine Corps, Navy, and Air Force lifted off for the first landing zone at WALL SOUTH.

With Chief Warrant Officer Michael J. Novosel, U.S. Army Retired at the controls, the lead chopper for the documentary, *In the Shadow of the Blade,* landed on the grounds in front of WALL SOUTH.

Within moments of setting down at Veterans Memorial Park, Vietnam veterans and park visitors rushed forward for a closer look and to shake hands with a true American hero...Chief Warrant Officer Michael J. Novosel

Medal of Honor recipient Chief Warrant Officer Michael J. Novosel (center) and two of his crew exit their helo at WALL SOUTH to speak with members of the media

**WALL SOUTH founders Lenny Collins and Nelson Wellborn are inter-
viewed for the 2004 Discovery channel's television documentary**
"In the Shadow of the Blade"

**Retired Navy Captain
Robert Rasmussen
poses alongside his sea
service statue of the
World War II Memorial.**

**Right, the World War II
Memorial as seen by
visitors facing the WALL**

Navy Seamen Habbah O'Connor (left) and Alysha Haran unveil the women's home front statue during the dedication of the World War II Memorial at Veterans Memorial Park.

A young visitor to Veterans Memorial Park gets a close up view of what a great grandfather he may have never known may have looked like.

Additional memorials at Veterans Memorial Park require extra beautifi-cation and maintenance, most of which is provided by volunteers like Virginia Dominck and Judy Birdwell, from the Azalea Garden Club, and other Pensacola area civic groups.

Volunteer maintenance has played a prominent role in maintaining the park right from the very beginning. For more than 20 years military personnel have stood at the ready to provide maintenance duty whenever called up to ensure that the park honoring their comrades in arms, will always be a showcase for locals and visitors.

Sailors from Corry Station volunteered to cut the grass and perform other chores in 1993 to ensure that the park would be ship shape for the dedication of the Huey helicopter.

Twenty-two years, Chief Petty Officer selectees from Corry Station and the Pensacola Naval Air Station, as part of their promotion ritual, clean bronze plaques at Veterans Memorial Park commemorating the War on Terrorism

This memorial, like the Vietnam memorial and World War II memorial was also met with skepticism and much debate before a final design was agreed upon. Some veterans of that war favored a traditional statute of an American Soldier. Others insisted on an oriental style arch. Still others opted for a memorial which portrayed not only the combat role of American involvement in Korea but also the humanitarian role.

Randy New's original design proposal for a Koran War Memorial

Finally a design proposed by Randy New, showing both the combat and humanitarian roles American troops played in Korea was chosen.

The Korean War Memorial was dedicated May 26, 2007.

New's Korean War Memorial features both the combat role of Americans in Korea (above) and the humanitarian role (left)

As part of their promotion ritual, Navy Chief Petty Officer selectees for 2015, from Corry Station and the Pensacola Naval Air Station, take a break from their Korean Memorial cleaning assignment to learn a little of the history of the "Forgotten War"

PARK TO HONOR ALL VETERANS

With the passage of time additional memorials and plaques, honoring the men and women of America's Armed Forces and the hardships and sacrifices they made to ensure America's freedoms, have been added. Pensacola, the State of Florida, and indeed the nation, can take great pride in the fact that a small band of determined Vietnam veterans, who was once referred to by a retired naval officer, as a "butch of rag-tag misfits," refused to give up their dream to memorialize their brothers left behind in Vietnam.

Memorials added over the years include a submarine memorial dedicated to the Submarine Lifeguard League, a special submarine unit of the Silent Service, placed in service at the start of the Gilbert Islands campaign in 1943.

Its assignment was to patrol close inshore during aerial bombardment of enemy held islands to rescue the crews of aircraft shot down while in the target area.

The pride of underwater service is portrayed in Veterans Memorial Park by the Silent Service Memorial

According to official Navy records 504 Aviators were rescued including the 41st President of the United States George H.W. Bush.

Many of these rescues were conducted under heavy enemy fire which gravely endangered the submarines and their crews. Certainly not the most popular duty assignment among submarine crews, but when they received a rescue assignment, the underwater warriors simply replied with an "Aye, Aye, Sir" and carried out their mission.

Chief Petty Officer selectees help ensure that the Pride of the Deep Memorial maintains it glow

The Purple Heart, American's oldest military combat award still in existence is awarded in the name of the President of the United States to any member of the Armed Forces of the United States who is wounded or killed, while serving in any capacity with any branch of the Armed Services.

Several of the Vietnam veterans responsible for the development of WALL SOUTH are recipients of the Purple Heart. One in particular Nelson Wellborn, lost a leg in Vietnam.

Others from that small band of WALL SOUTH founders, and thousands of other Vietnam veterans across the nation are still recovering from physical and mental injuries as a of result of combat service in Vietnam.

The Purple Heart Memorial is a symbol of courage and dedication in the face of mortal danger

The Huey helicopter destroyed by Hurricane Ivan in 2004 was replaced in 2007 with a Cobra helicopter. Though the Cobra too, played an important role in Vietnam, for most Vietnam veterans, however, it was the distinctive whup, whup, whup, of the Huey's rotor blades that they associate with Vietnam service.

The AH-1G Cobra was first deployed to Vietnam in September 1967. Its primary mission was to provide fire support for the troop carrying Hueys. The Cobra also provided ground commanders with air superiority without having to call in the Air Force. Its narrow airframe presented a much more difficult target than the UH-1 Huey.

During the Vietnam War, the AH-1G Cobra was used in a variety of missions ranging from armed escort and reconnaissance to fire suppression and aerial rocket artillery.

In August 2012, a clock tower, known as the Marine Aviation Memorial Bell,

May Peace Be in Our Homes and Communities

May Peace Prevail on Earth

Like its predecessor the Huey, the Cobra was quickly accepted by the public as a welcome attraction to Veterans Memorial Park, and like the Huey, it serves as a landmark for visitors visiting the Park for the first time was added to the park commemorating 100 years of Marine Corps aviation and honoring all aviation marines.

Standing thirty feet tall the tower features a 250-pound bronze bell, which symbolizes the bells used in Marine aviation units to sound the call to action when word was received that ground forces were in need of air support.

Marine Aviation Memorial Tower

The Marine Aviation Memorial Tower pays tribute to the men and women of America who swore an oath to defend their nation by serving with Marine Aviation in all warfare specialties, including those Marines who maintain, crew, control and support Marine Aviation training and operations. It is dedicated to all who have made the ultimate sacrifice in service to America.

After the attack on the World Trade Center in 2011, attention shifted to the veterans of another kind of war. The War on Terrorism.

Twelve bronze plaques commemorating the War on Terrorism are displayed at the Romana Street entrance to Veterans Memorial Park

In an effort to honor American veterans engaged in this new type of warfare a Global War on Terrorism subcommittee was formed.

As Congressman Jeff Miller stated at a dedication ceremony, Northwest Florida is steeped in military tradition and enriched with a strong military presence. The full range of service, sacrifice, duty and honor that comes with military service is amply illustrated in the example of our own citizens.

We in turn honor that service at Veterans Memorial Park with monuments already established and others yet to come. This park is dedicated to the memories of those who have died in the service of our country, whether in time of war or in peacetime.

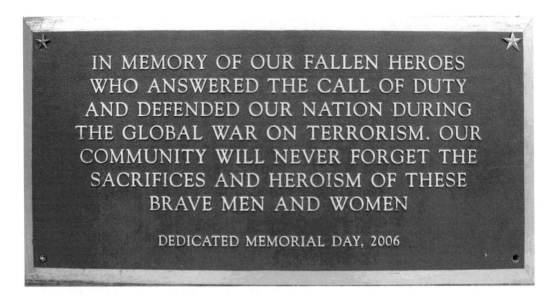

IN MEMORY OF OUR FALLEN HEROES
WHO ANSWERED THE CALL OF DUTY
AND DEFENDED OUR NATION DURING
THE GLOBAL WAR ON TERRORISM. OUR
COMMUNITY WILL NEVER FORGET THE
SACRIFICES AND HEROISM OF THESE
BRAVE MEN AND WOMEN

DEDICATED MEMORIAL DAY, 2006

CPL JONATHAN R. SPEARS, USMC
KIA - OCTOBER 23, 2005
OPERATION IRAQI FREEDOM

SSGT DANIEL J. CLAY, USMC
KIA - DECEMBER 1, 2005
OPERATION IRAQI FREEDOM

SSGT MARLON HARPER, USA
KIA - APRIL 21, 2007
OPERATION IRAQI FREEDOM

CPL JOSEPH N. LANDRY III
KIA - SEPTEMBER 19, 2007
OPERATION IRAQI FREEDOM

PFC KEVIN J. ELLENBURG, USA
KIA - NOVEMBER 1, 2006
OPERATION IRAQI FREEDOM

SGT DANIEL L. MCCALL, USA
KIA - OCTOBER 30, 2007
OPERATION IRAQI FREEDOM

SSG JAVARES J. WASHINGTON, USA
FEBRUARY 11, 2008
OPERATION IRAQI FREEDOM

SSG DARRIS J. DAWSON, US ARMY
SEPTEMBER 14, 2008
OPERATION IRAQI FREEDOM

L/CPL TRAVIS NELSON, USMC
KIA - AUGUST 18, 2011
OPERATION ENDURING FREEDOM

PFC MATTHEW C. COLIN, USA
KIA - NOVEMBER 16, 2011
OPERATION ENDURING FREEDOM

STAFF SERGEANT JESSE L. THOMAS, JR, USA
KIA - JUNE 10, 2013
OPERATION ENDURING FREEDOM

Congressman Miller stated that other memorials will undoubtedly be erected on the site of this former baseball park as time passes and space permits. The latest, as of this writing, was a memorial, erected by the Florida Society of Sons of American Revolution honoring Eighteenth Century Revolutionary War veterans—the Minutemen.

Vietnam Veterans Motorcycle Club Honor Guard and Congressman Jeff Miller (rear) march to WALL SOUTH to place a wreath at the Wall in honor of all deceased American veterans. The wreath placement was part of Memorial Day services at WALL SOUTH.

Revolutionary War Memorial at the Romana Street entrance to
Veterans Memorial Park

What stated as one young Marine veteran's dream to pay homage to a high school friend and the 58, 272 other Americans who died in Vietnam, has evolved into A MUST SEE Northwest Florida attraction for residents and visitors alike. It has become hallowed ground, much like a cemetery dedicated to veterans of all wars.

Despite the addition of other memorials over the years and possibly more to follow, the heart of this magnificent park, remains WALL SOUTH.

Here, are listed the names of young Americans from all 50 states, District of Columba, Puerto Rico, and the U.S. Virgin Islands, who paid the ultimate sacrifice in the name of freedom.

The author's home state of West Virginia suffered the highest casualty rate, per capita, in the nation with 711 souls. Fourteen of them were from his hometown of Bluefield, West Virginia.

This former weed and insect-infected ballpark not only pays homage to those who gave their life in the name of freedom, but has become a peaceful sanctuary where people can gather, visit with

Old sailors visit the WALL to reunite with lost shipmates and bring them up to date on the current state of the world.

loved ones and stroll among the memorials without fear of showing signs of any weakness or emotions.

The World War II Memorial provides youngsters with an opportunity to reach out and touch a bronze figure at the World War II Memorial and dream of a grandfather they never had a chance to know.

The Korean War Memorial reminds us that freedom is not free. Though short in duration, Korean claimed the lives of 36, 574 American service members and ended in a draw.

Vietnam era veterans, while searching for a name can look at their reflection in the WALL and feel they have been united with those whose names are engraved in the shiny black granite.

Long retired seafarers can relive and snigger at the sea stories they and their shipmates told and re-told while deployed for upwards to nine months at time aboard one of the Navy's mighty aircraft carriers, cruisers, destroyers or auxiliary vessels—tankers, ammunition and stories ships.

To visit WALL SOUTH is to become a part of the Wall

The Wall offers the perfect setting for proud grandfathers to introduce their grandchildren to lost friends listed on the black granite panels of WALL SOUTH, in the hope that their children will never have to go to war

Military spouses discuss the problems faced by military families during a visit to Veterans Memorial Park

WALL SOUTH/Veterans Memorial Park is often a source of tranquility for military spouses to meet and discuss their latest books or club activities.

Benches sponsored by patriotic organizations and placed in front of WALL SOUTH provide more than a place to rest—they also serve as a reminder that the freedoms Americans take for granted carry a huge price tag and many are painfully reminded of this each time they visit the park

Former Pensacola Mayor Vince Whibbs and Medal of Honor recipient Sammy Davis share an emotional moment during Memorial Day services at WALL SOUTH, May 29, 2005.

A mother/den leader points out the name of a loved one killed in Vietnam during a Veterans Day visit to WALL SOUTH.

Finally locating the name of a loved one can be tough on the entire family

After nearly half a century, people still find it hard to believe that more than fifty thousand Americans lost their life in a country few had ever heard of before 1960

Miniature American flags atop the black granite panels of WALL SOUTH never fail to build strong emotions

**On warm days visitors to WALL SOUTH often have to be creative
when looking for a place to find a little shade**

Over the years, leaving medals, notes and cards and other items, at the base of **WALL SOUTH** has become a tradition for visitors to Veterans Memorial Park.

The top of WALL SOUTH was the perfect observation point for documenting the dedication of the World War II Memorial

Motorcycle clubs have been making an annual bike ride to Veterans Memorial Park for Memorial Day and Veterans Day Services since the park was dedicated in 1992.

An emotional prayer for a buddy on the WALL

The search for the name of missing family member, friend or fellow Vietnam Veteran never ends. Many visitors to the WALL SOUTH photograph the panel containing special names

Veterans Memorial Park continues to grow and with each passing year and ceremony recognizing the sacrifices made by American men and women in uniform, the crowds seem to grow larger with more and more people visiting the park to show their appreciation and pay their respects to those left behind, whether it was during World War II, Korean or Vietnam, honoring those whose sacrifice gave Americans a nation worth defending. The next gap to be filled will be a memorial to honor the current generation of Americans who are fighting the Global War on Terror. The form that this memorial will eventually take is in the process of being determined. However, the time for a new memorial has clearly arrived.

With each new service honoring America's armed services, the crowd grows larger and as in the past, the WALL is generally the main attraction.

A lone protestor exercises his rights, as guaranteed by those who died to ensure them.

While most visitors to Veterans Memorial Park are there to honor those who have made the ultimate sacrifice for America, regrettably, an occasional protestor will also make an appearance.

Though he/she may be viewed with contempt by veterans and loved ones of those who didn't return, this sort of visitor, is also welcome at Veterans Memorial Park. Hopefully they will come to realize, that their right to protest is a direct result of the sacrifices the men and women the park was built to memorialize, gave their life to ensure.

From its inception in 1992, WALL SOUTH and Veterans Memorial Park has undergone numerous governmental changes. As of this writing the park is governed by a volunteer Board of Directors by license agreement with the City of Pensacola. There are no salaries or other forms of financial compensation. The goal of the Foundation is to operate the Park in such a manner that no tax-payer funds are expended in its care and maintenance.

The park was originally constructed in a similar manner, funded solely by grants and donations. Veterans Memorial Park continues to depend on the donations of those who love and support it and revere the memory of those honored there.

Protestors or not, Memorial and Veterans Day ceremonies continue to attract huge crowds ranging in age from toddlers to senior citizens. Regardless of the event, the glossy black granite panels of WALL SOUTH and the 58,272 names engraved on the WALL are the main attraction.

The WALL provides the opportunity to visit with loved ones, which many people born after 1975 never had a chance to meet.

The author's granddaughter, Madelyn, pays her respects to the men and women listed on the WALL.
Below, she seems to be offering her condolences to the little girl of the Children's Homecoming Memorial.

All Americans born between 1917 and 2015 have known war in one form or another. If they didn't personally wear an American military uniform, chances are a family member, or someone they knew did. The cost of being able to live in free country has been extremely high.

During World War I: 1917-1918— the War to end all Wars—116,516 Americans died in defense of America. Twenty-three years later, thousands of Americans were once again called up to go in harm's way to ensure the American way of life. Between 1941 and 1945, 405,399 Americans paid the ultimate sacrifice during four years of bloody fighting in World War II.

Five short years later American warriors, many of them veterans of World War II, plus hundreds of a newer generation were

World War I claimed the lives of 116,516 Americans

once again called upon to take up arms in defense of another foreign nation— Korea.

The Korean War: 1950-1953—began as a civil war between north and South Korea, but the conflict soon became international when, under U.S. leadership, the United Nations went to the aid of

405,399 died during World War II

South Korea, after China joined the dispute on the side of North Korea, thus creating a divided Korea and the start of the cold war in Asia. On July 27, 1953, an armistice was signed bringing an end to hostilities, but the armistice was only a ceasefire agreement, not a formal peace treaty ending the war. Despite the fact that the United States, with the backing of the United Nations, had intervened in another countries dispute between neighbors America finally withdrew without a victory or defeat.

Eight years later America was once again involved in a dispute between Asian neighbors—North and South Vietnam.

The Vietnam War: 1961-1975 claimed the lives of 58,219 Americans during more than a decade of warfare.

What has been called America's most "unpopular war"; Vietnam resulted in the loss of respect for American's Armed Forces and the loss of 58,272 American men and women

The so-called Forgotten War took another 36,574 American lives.

The first major foreign crisis for the United States after the end of the Cold War presented itself in August 1990 when the Iraqi army invaded the tiny country of Kuwait, an American ally and a major supplier of oil to the United States. The Iraqi takeover posed an immediate threat to neighboring Saudi Arabia, another major exporter of oil. If Saudi Arabia fell to Iraq it would control one-fifth of the world's oil supply. The first Gulf War—Operation Desert Storm—lasted less than a year and took the lives of 292 American troops.

After a twelve-year period of relative calmness America's armed forces were once again called upon to take up arms following the September 11, 2001, attack on America when militant Islamic fundamentalist terrorists hijacked commercial airliners and flew them into the World Trade Center and the Pentagon, killing nearly 3,000 people.

On March 19, 2003 with incomplete reports about Iraq's Weapons of Mass Destruction capabilities and the support of a small contingent of international supporters, President George W. Bush gave the green light to launch Operation Iraqi Freedom.

The second President Bush told Americans that Iraq was the next target in an ongoing worldwide battle against terrorism that had begun with America's attack on Afghanistan's Taliban government in September 2001. The president warned that "helping Iraqis achieve a united, stable and free country would require a sustained U.S. commitment."

The President received harsh criticism for the war. Critics claimed his administration primarily sought control of Iraq's vast oil resources, or that the war was in retaliation for an attempt on former President George H.W. Bush's life, ordered by Iraqi President Saddam Hussein, in 1990.

Although bush announced "mission accomplished" and the end of combat operations on May 1, 2003, Iraq continued to experience ongoing deadly attacks by insurgents while U.S. and coalition troops and civilian contractors attempted to establish an Iraqi army and police force and establish a freely elected government.

In the first four years of the war, American casualties stood at more than 3,000 with more than 23,000 wounded.

Over the years, WALL SOUTH and Veterans Memorial Park has become a magnet for veterans groups, active duty personnel and others wanting to re-unite with fellow veterans and present-day service members.

Veterans and active duty service members come together at Veterans Memorial park to honor those who have made the ultimate sacrifice in defense of their country.

A visitor to WALL SOUTH during a Memorial Day ceremony, scans a copy of the original WALL SOUTH book published in 1995.

Corporal Garrett Glassman, USMC; CPO Art Giberson, USN Ret.; former Lance Corporal Lenny Collins, USMC; and Lieutenant Colonel David Glassman, USMC Ret., take a moment to show their service pride and to honor those who never returned from wartime service, during a Memorial Day service at Veterans Memorial Park

While Veterans Memorial Park has become a prime tourist attraction, more importantly it has become a site for veterans of recent wars to gather and have photos taken with family members and friends who now wear the uniform.

Family of Warriors:
Vietnam veteran Chief Petty Officer Art Giberson, Ret., with grandson PFC Nick
Giberson, Operation Iraqi Freedom and son Senior Chief Petty Officer, Ret., Operation
Storm, pose for a family photo at Veterans Memorial Park

Each service at Veterans Memorial Park actually starts long before the first guest arrives with volunteers getting the park ready.

A young mother helps her son place flags on top the Wall South Vietnam Veterans Memorial to honor the nation's veterans during the 2015 Veterans Day ceremony at Veterans

Veterans Day 2015, while slightly smaller than previous observances, was nevertheless special and sober paying special homage to two servicemen killed in Afghanistan.

Veterans Day 2015, like the first one 23 years earlier was a combination family and patriotism day. In addition to honoring those lost in previous conflicts it was also a time honor two Pensacola-area service members, Staff Sgt. Forrest Sibley and Senior Airman Nathan Sartain, two local American heroes, who paid the ultimate sacrifice while serving in Afghanistan.

Plaques honoring Sibley and Sartain will were placed at the Romana Street entrance to Veterans Memorial along with the twelve placed there earlier and there is little doubt that additional plaques will placed there in the future.

An Air Force Honor Guard parades plaques with the names Staff Sgt. Forrest B. Sibley, USAF and Senior Airman Nathan Sartain, USAF before family members at Veterans Memorial Park on Veterans Day 2015

Tears flow freely as an Air Force Honor Guard presents latest Global War on Terrorism to family members at Veterans Memorial Park

A new memorial beach, sponsored by the Combat Veterans Motorcycle Association was unveiled at Veterans Memorial Park on Veterans Day 2015

As the final pages of this memorial narrative are being written, the men and women of America's Armed Forces continue to go in harm's way in the name of freedom in places such as Afghanistan, Pakistan and Syria. These men and women can take pride in the fact that before many of them were even born, a small band of veterans from another era were fighting to build a Veterans Memorial in the Florida Panhandle town that former Pensacola Mayor Vince Whibbs referred to as "The Gateway to the Sunshine State."

As stated earlier, the site chosen for this memorial to America's defenders of freedom was once a popular Pensacola attraction known as Admiral Mason Park, a 2,000-seat minor league baseball stadium situated on the Pensacola Bay waterfront. Due to the unpleasant odors from a nearby wastewater treatment plant, the park quickly acquired the nickname of "Stinko Stadium." After the league folded in 1962 for refusing to accept African-American players, Admiral Mason Park languished for nearly two decades before ultimately being demolished.

Veterans Memorial Park is located on the site of a former minor league baseball Park.

By the time the City of Pensacola appropriated 5.5 acres of the site to be used for a half-scale replica of the Vietnam Veterans Memorial, Stinko Stadium had deteriorated to little more than an overgrown, weed infested eyesore, which the city turned over to what one city councilman referred to as "A bunch of rag-tag cry babies" (Vietnam veterans) for construction of WALL SOUTH.

That smelly old site has since become known as Veterans Memorial Park and is now home to several other veteran memorial monuments.

The remaining section of the former baseball park, still retaining the name of retired Vice Admiral Charles P. Mason, a former two time mayor of Pensacola has been transformed, into a beautiful two-acre pond, with fountains, walkways, and benches. The extensive landscaping includes live oak trees, magnolias, crepe myrtles, and sabal palms— creating a scenic setting for a picnic, enjoying the beautiful weather and great views of Pensacola Bay.

These two parks double as a place to pay homage to those who have, and are continuing, to serve our great nation. Whether it's a visit to Pensacola's Veterans Memorial Park for a memorial service or a leisurely stroll around the beautifully landscaped pond of Admiral Mason Park, we should never forget the visit of the Moving Wall to Pensacola in the winter of 1987 and a pledge made by one battle-scarred Vietnam veteran to build a memorial in honor of his buddies who never returned from Southeast Asia.

**Two time Mayor of Pensacola,
Vice Admiral Charles P. Mason**

Entrance to Admiral Mason Park

The fountains of Admiral Mason Park provide a pictorial foreground for Veterans Memorial Park

About the Author

Art Giberson, a retired Navy Chief Petty Officer, made two deployments to Vietnam as a combat photographer and is one of the originators of the Pensacola, Florida
Vietnam Veterans Memorial.

A native of Bluefield, West Virginia the Chief and his wife, Stella, reside in Pensacola, Florida, near their children and grandchildren.

In addition to *Veterans Memorial Park* Chief Giberson has produced four other pictorial history books: *The Blue Ghost*, *Wall South*, *Eyes of the Fleet* and, *Freedom's First Responder*.

Art Giberson